KEELBOAT ANNIE

Designed by Susan and Dave Albers

LEGENDS OF THE WORLD

KEELBOAT ANNIE

• AN AFRICAN-AMERICAN LEGEND •

RETOLD BY JANET P. JOHNSON   ILLUSTRATED BY CHARLES REASONER

Have you ever heard about Annie Christmas? If you're from Louisiana you may have, because that's where Annie made her home. But for those of you who don't know her, listen up and listen well—there's a lot to tell! For here is how she got her nickname, Keelboat Annie.

Annie Christmas was the strongest, biggest, bravest woman who ever lived. Ask anyone who knew her, and they'll tell you the same.

Annie came into the world on Christmas day, all twenty-five pounds of her. Her parents knew she was special right from the start. Her skin was dark as ebony, her raven curls grew wild around her face, and her black eyes shone bright as polished coal. She was a strong baby—and smart, too! Annie hadn't been in her cradle a minute when she said, "Howdy, Mama." Then out of the cradle that baby hopped. To everyone's surprise, Annie swung her mama up in her arms and twirled the woman around and around.

As time passed, Annie kept on growing stronger and bigger. She loved to run races with the other girls and boys, but they were no match for her. So instead she raced the fastest horses in town. And she beat them, too!

Annie lived near the Mississippi River. During quiet times, she loved to sit on shore and watch the mighty, muddy waters flowing to the sea.

One special day Annie caught sight of a paddleboat chugging down the river. She jumped into the water and started racing alongside the boat. Annie beat the boat to the dock by a mile.

Pulling herself up out of the water, Annie laughed a roaring good laugh. "That was fun," she said. "Someday I'd like to work on this river!"

And that's just what Annie did. When she was about sixteen years old, she told her parents, "Mama and Papa, I love you dearly, but it's time for me to go." Annie's parents didn't try to talk her out of leaving. They would miss Annie, but they knew she was as strong-minded as she was able-bodied. By this time she weighed 250 pounds and stood close to seven feet tall.

So Annie's mama helped her sew some sturdy overalls. Her papa gave her his favorite hat to keep the rain off. Then Annie tied a bright red kerchief around her neck. She was ready.

Waving good-bye, Annie set off for New Orleans to look for work. When Annie got to that bustling city, she went straight to the docks and applied for the job of longshoreman. She'd heard about the hard-working men who loaded and unloaded cargo boxes onto and off of the boats there. To Annie, it sounded like an easy job.

Unfortunately, the foreman, who wasn't known for his good manners, didn't agree. He took one look at Annie and snorted, "This ain't no job for a woman."

Annie was a patient soul, but nothing made her madder than to hear about what she *couldn't* do! Right then and there, she challenged the man to some arm wrestling, but the foreman wouldn't hear of it. "Go home, crazy woman," he said.

Annie's dark eyes glittered angrily. Then she had an idea. The next morning, she put on her overalls and a big, baggy shirt. She tied her hair up in the red kerchief, and she pulled her father's floppy hat down over her eyes.

Back to the docks Annie marched. Hoisting a huge crate, she balanced it on her head. Then she grabbed a bale of cotton in one arm and a barrel of nails in the other. Easily carrying the heavy load, she sauntered past the foreman.

The man's eyes bulged from his head when he saw such strength! "Sir," he said, addressing Annie, "would you happen to be looking for a job? I could use a man like you."

Annie grinned and accepted his offer. All that day she worked, carrying more crates, bales, and boxes than anyone had ever seen. At last, the foreman called the other longshoremen over. "When each of you can do the work that this one can, you can call yourselves men!" he said.

When she heard that, Annie couldn't keep a straight face. Her laughter boomed like a foghorn across the river. She tore off her hat and kerchief. "Or maybe you can call yourselves women!" she chuckled. "Remember me?"

The foreman certainly did remember her. He turned as red as a rooster's comb when the other men burst out laughing. But he was so impressed with Annie's strength, he never told her to go home again.

Annie soon became famous up and down the river for her size, her strength, and her big heart. People loved her, and she loved them right back. The one thing Annie couldn't stand was a bully. She faced plenty of them to defend her friends—and she whipped those bullies good. In fact, each time Annie fought, she always knocked out one of the bully's teeth. She strung the teeth on a necklace, like pretty white pearls. Many folks say that necklace was twenty feet long!

All along the Mississippi, people knew of Annie's bravery. For when storm clouds gathered over the city of New Orleans, as they often did, they brought rain and terrible floods.

At those times, Annie worked alongside the men, hauling bags of sand to the riverbank to raise a levee to hold the raging flood waters back. When all the others quit, exhausted, Annie worked on alone, late into the night. She was determined to save the town she loved from being washed clear away.

The longer Annie lived in New Orleans, the better she came to know the ins and outs of the Mississippi River. One of her keenest ambitions was to become the captain of her very own keelboat. These boats were used to carry cargo down the river. Annie loved to imagine herself cruising free on the water.

One fine day, Annie saw the chance to make her dream come true. She knew a rich man who lived five miles above New Orleans, in a town called Foggy Marsh. This man owned several keelboats, and he was very fond of betting. "Sir," Annie told the man, "I'll wager I can pole a keelboat faster than any ten of your keelboat captains put together. And to make things interesting, I'll beat them going both downstream and upstream! If I win, you'll give me one of your keelboats.
If you win, I'll work
for you with no
wages for
a year."

The man knew Annie well. He knew that if the race was only downstream from Foggy Marsh to New Orleans, Annie was sure to win. But to race back from New Orleans upstream to Foggy Marsh was another matter. The strong currents were impossible for one man to row against. But with ten of his men against Annie, he might have a chance of winning. "You're on!" he said, shaking Annie's hand.

News of the wager soon spread. On the day of the race, spectators lined the banks of the river, eager to see what Annie would do. A cannon boomed to signal the start of the race. Off the two keelboats sped, with Annie in the lead.

Five miles downriver, the boats reached New Orleans. It was time to turn around. Annie easily turned her boat, but she struggled to make headway against the mighty current. When she looked back, Annie saw the ten men in the other boat. They were gaining on her!

Without a second thought, Annie tied one end of a rope to her keelboat and the other end around her waist. Then she jumped into the swirling waters, climbed onto the riverbank, and started running as fast as she could, pulling her boat behind her. Soon the keelboat was flying upstream. Amid cheers and howls of delight, Annie won the race! That's how she became a keelboat captain. From then on, she was known as Keelboat Annie.

That race was also how Annie met the man she would marry. Lucky Charlie was a fine gentleman who had watched the whole race. He was mighty impressed by Annie's great spirit. Because he always loved a long shot, he had bet all his money on Annie. After the race, he ran up to her and proclaimed his love. And when Annie realized how much Charlie believed in her, she knew she loved him, too.

Lucky Charlie and Annie got hitched and made a happy couple. In time, they had twelve handsome sons, all seven feet tall with ebony skin like their mother's. Some folks say all twelve boys were born one after the other on the same day.

Times were happy, but one day when Charlie was playing poker, tragedy struck. He was dealt a royal flush, and in his excitement, his heart gave out. The other players felt so bad about the situation, they gave all Charlie's winnings plus their own to Annie and the boys. But it was little consolation. Annie grieved for a long time.

24

Finally, some of Annie's friends stopped by. "Annie," one of them said, "it's time you stopped moping. Lucky Charlie loved your spirit of adventure. He wouldn't want to see you this way."

In her heart, Annie knew her friend was right. So she proposed that she and the other ladies take a pleasure cruise on the Mississippi. Her friends agreed.

Each woman dressed in her finest clothes. Annie stuck long feathers in her hair and put on her fanciest purple dress. Looking very lovely, the ladies set out for fun on Annie's keelboat. At each port, one of the ladies was met by a gentleman, who invited her to join him for dinner. One by one, Annie's friends left, until she was all by herself.

"Oh well," said Annie, looking up at the stars, "it's lovely and peaceful being out on the river."

Suddenly, Annie spotted one of the finest, most prettily painted paddleboats she had ever seen. She poled over to it, lashed the keelboat to the larger boat, and climbed aboard. The paddleboat was called the *Stormy Queen*. It was the fanciest boat on the river, filled with velvet couches, fine paintings, and golden, carved woodwork.

Annie was relaxing and enjoying the luxury when she noticed dark clouds racing past the moon. Within minutes a storm had rolled in. A bolt of lightning streaked across the sky, and deafening thunder filled the passengers' ears.

Annie knew the boat should head for port. The captain knew it, too. But in his haste, he decided to try a new cutoff on the river. Cutoffs were shortcuts through the twisting banks of the Mississippi. These paths were dangerously narrow even on calm days. At night, in bad weather, they were full of peril.

Annie warned the captain, "Don't take the cutoff. Let me handle the boat. I know every inch of this river."

The captain grew angry. "I'm in charge here. And if you don't like it, may the devil take you!"

As if the devil had heard his words, the boat began to shake and twist. It was caught on the stump of a tree that had been left in the cutoff!

"Come with me," Annie urged the passengers. She hurried them onto her keelboat. Then she poled out into the main channel of the river and into the storm. Behind them the passengers heard the paddleboat shudder and crack. In one huge gulp, the river swallowed it up.

Annie fought both the river and the storm with
every ounce of strength she had. At last, she brought
everyone to safety. But the effort had been too great,
even for Annie. She collapsed on shore and died that
very night.

Annie's sons gathered around their beloved mother. The next day, they dressed her in a black gown and laid her in an ebony coffin. They placed her coffin upon a fine hearse pulled by beautiful black horses. Annie's sons walked alongside the hearse. Behind them came hundreds of Annie's friends from up and down the river.

When the hearse neared the river, Annie's sons put her on a grand black barge. The crowd watched as the river carried brave Annie away. They knew they would never forget her or her courageous deeds. And they never have!

To this day, folks say that if you look out at the river on a misty night, you just might see Annie, floating on her barge to the sea.

African-American history traces its beginnings back to Africa, where millions of Africans were captured to be brought to the Americas as slaves. However, not all people of color in the United States were slaves. Some were indentured servants—people who had to work for a master for a set period of time, after which they would be freed.

Before the end of the Civil War, some estimate, ten percent of the black population in America was free. A small number of free people of color became rich, owning land and ships. Most free blacks lived in the cities of the north. Yet New Orleans, the southern city in Louisiana where *Keelboat Annie* takes place, was a city where many free people of color lived and worked, some as keelboat operators, just like Annie. Ironically, New Orleans was also one of the main slave markets of the South.

Being "free" did not provide equal rights for blacks. Free African-Americans always had to carry papers to prove their freedom. They were not allowed to vote, to own firearms, or to move about at will without a pass in certain cities.

Despite these conditions, many free African-Americans accomplished great things. Some became doctors; others started newspapers, schools, and universities; and yet others founded churches.

Folktales—stories handed down by word of mouth from generation to generation—flourished in the African-American culture of those times. Tall tales about Annie Christmas have been told in New Orleans for more than a hundred years. Interestingly, tales about this larger-than-life folk hero also exist in Irish-American folklore, in which Annie is a white heroine.

Some believe the character of Annie is based on a real black woman. Whatever its origin, the tale of Annie Christmas is full of adventure, humor, and sadness. Annie also has a unique place in folklore because of her status as a strong, female African-American character, one of the few to be found among the heroes of tall tales.